cultivate

GROWING IN SPIRITUAL
DISCIPLINES JESUS'S WAY

© 2022 Lifeway Press®
Reprinted June 2022

No part of this work may be reproduced or transmitted in any form or by any means, electronic or mechanical, including photocopying and recording, or by any information storage or retrieval system, except as may be expressly permitted in writing by the publisher. Requests for permission should be addressed in writing to Lifeway Press®, 200 Powell Place, Suite 100, Brentwood, TN 37027-7514.

ISBN 978-1-0877-4831-3
Item 005833489
Dewey Decimal Classification Number: 242
Subject Heading: DEVOTIONAL LITERATURE / BIBLE STUDY AND TEACHING / GOD

Printed in the United States of America

Student Ministry Publishing
Lifeway Resources
200 Powell Place, Suite 100
Brentwood, TN 37027-7514

We believe that the Bible has God for its author; salvation for its end; and truth, without any mixture of error, for its matter and that all Scripture is totally true and trustworthy. To review Lifeway's doctrinal guideline, please visit www.lifeway.com/doctrinalguideline.

Unless otherwise noted, all Scripture quotations are taken from the Christian Standard Bible®, Copyright © 2017 by Holman Bible Publishers. Used by permission. Christian Standard Bible® and CSB® are federally registered trademarks of Holman Bible Publishers.

publishing team

Director, Student Ministry
Ben Trueblood

Manager, Student Ministry Publishing
John Paul Basham

Editorial Team Leader
Karen Daniel

Writer
Angela Sanders

Content Editor
Stephanie Cross

Production Editor
Brooke Hill

Graphic Designer
Kaitlin Redmond

TABLE OF CONTENTS

4
intro

5
getting started

6
inward disciplines

40
outward disciplines

74
corporate disciplines

108
how to journal your prayers

110
why we need space for solitude (and why it's okay)

INTRO

Imagine a library. Picture the shelves upon shelves filled with books. There are leather bound books, paperback books, reference books, children's books, the greatest works of fiction, and biographies of the most interesting people who have ever lived. If you wanted to learn while at the library, you would grab some books, find a comfy chair, sit down, and start reading.

Now, imagine you just moved to a new town. At your new school, in your very first class, the girl sitting next to you says, "Hey, I know you're new in town. If you need help, just let me know." She's wearing a graphic tee of your favorite band, has the cute scrunchie you saw on TikTok® last week, and a volleyball by her feet. You'd probably strike up a conversation, feeling like you'd just met your new best friend.

Both of these scenarios resemble your spiritual life in a way. If you want to learn and grow, you have to spend time doing things that will help you learn and grow. If you want to get to know Jesus better, you have to spend time with Him. These things that help us grow and spend time with Jesus are called spiritual disciplines.

Since Jesus models godly living for us, it's helpful to see how He both practiced and taught spiritual disciplines. That's what this book will do. Over the next thirty days, we'll explore what Jesus had to say about prayer, fasting, worship, and much more. We'll get a front row seat to how our Savior actually did the things He taught us to do. Along the way, we'll also learn and grow in our relationship with Jesus, cultivating habits that will help us continue on this journey for the rest of our lives.

GETTING STARTED

This devotional contains thirty days of content, broken down into sections. Each day is divided into three elements—discover, delight, and display—to help you answer core questions related to Scripture.

discover |

This section helps you examine the passage in light of who God is and determine what it says about your identity in relationship to Him. Included here is the daily Scripture reading, focus passage, along with illustrations and commentary to guide you as you explore God's Word.

delight |

In this section, you'll be challenged by questions and activities that help you see how God is alive and active in every detail of His Word and your life. We've given you a whole page to write your answers to these questions, so really think and dig in.

display |

Here's where you take action. Display calls you to apply what you've learned through each day's devotion.

> **Each day also includes a prayer activity at the conclusion of the devotion.**

Throughout the devotional, you'll also find other resources to help you connect with the topic, such as Scripture memory verses, additional resources, and articles that help you go deeper into God's Word.

SECTION 1

Inward Disciplines

The first type of spiritual disciplines we'll explore are inward disciplines. When Jesus sets us free, we become brand new inside instantly. But it can take a while to understand what the new life God has given us is all about. Prayer, fasting, and studying God's Word—the Bible—help us get to know our heavenly Father better and understand what He expects from us.

DAY 1

So Worth It

discover |

READ LUKE 2:52.

*And Jesus increased in wisdom and stature, and
in favor with God and with people.*

Want to grow? Well, it doesn't just happen. Nothing and no one grows automatically—not even Jesus, the Son of God. For growth to happen, something has to be taken in and then applied.

For example, Jesus increased in stature—or grew up. So, we know He ate food, drank water, and slept, and we know His body used these things to stay healthy and mature. We can make the same assumptions about His spiritual growth. The Bible says Jesus increased in wisdom and in favor with God and people, so we know He went to God—who is the source of wisdom—to learn, and then used what He learned to obey God. As a result, God was glorified and pleased with Jesus and the people around Jesus, who probably benefited from His obedience and liked and respected Him. Isn't that what we all want?

Spiritual growth is incredibly simple, but not always easy. Jesus didn't do whatever He felt like doing in the moment and things just happened to work out. No, Jesus pursued God intentionally and consistently, no matter how He felt, who was near, or what was going on around Him. We call the methods He used spiritual disciplines because they require conscious effort: prayer, fasting, study of God's Word, simplicity, solitude, submission, service, corporate worship, stewardship, and fellowship. Fortunately for us, these disciplines are just as effective for pursuing God now as they were back then. In fact, they're absolutely necessary. We can't grow without them!

---

delight |

On a scale from one to ten, how would you rate the amount of thought and effort you put into pursuing God on a regular basis?

1	2	3	4	5	6	7	8	9	10
Zero				Some				I give it my all	

Taking this number into consideration, what degree of spiritual growth can you reasonably expect to have experienced so far?

What, if anything, needs to change?

display |

Read today's verse again. Without borrowing any of the words, write down what you hope people will be able to say about you when they look back on the life you lived. Consider how far you are willing to go to live this kind of life.

Now, go back through the list of spiritual disciplines below. Underline every spiritual discipline you have practiced before. Circle those you practice regularly. Put a star over those you consider personal strengths. Put an exclamation mark over those you need to work on or haven't considered before. Over the next month, use this devotional to make a plan to grow in your practice of spiritual disciplines.

Prayer, fasting, study of God's Word, simplicity, solitude, submission, service, corporate worship, stewardship, fellowship

Spend some time talking to God. Ask God to give you the desire to pursue Him like Jesus did. Thank Him for showing you how to find Him through Jesus's example. Commit to using what you learn from Him to obey Him so He will be glorified and pleased and so the people in your life will be blessed. Tell God He is worth anything it takes for you to grow spiritually.

DAY 2

Early in the Morning

discover |

READ MARK 1:35-38.

Very early in the morning, while it was still dark, [Jesus] got up, went out, and made his way to a deserted place; and there he was praying.
—Mark 1:35

Jesus never sinned. Can you even imagine? No bad deeds. No bad thoughts. No bad attitudes. Ever! Even when He got up early to pray. When we get up early for anything, we're likely to gripe that the sun isn't up yet and we shouldn't be either or tell people not to talk to us until we've at least had a cup of coffee. You might say, "Well, Jesus was perfect." Jesus is the Son of God, of course, but that doesn't mean He didn't struggle to resist sin. Scripture tells us He was tempted just like we are. That's what makes the fact that He never sinned so amazing!

So how did Jesus keep His heart, thoughts, attitudes, and actions lined up with God's will and character at all times? He prayed. He got alone with God and talked to Him on a regular basis, but not just to tell God what He was up to, what His needs were, and to ask for help—His Father already knew what He needed. Jesus also talked to God to enjoy His Father's company, offer Him praise, and receive instruction so He could keep doing and saying what God wanted Him to do and say the exact way God wanted Him to do and say it.

Rather than needing coffee or turning off the alarm for a little more sleep, Jesus started His day with prayer. This time helped Jesus serve the God He loved with excellence. None of us are sinless like Jesus, but we can love God with increasing excellence if we spend time getting to know who He is and what He expects—and we can do this through prayer.

delight |

Is your prayer life driven by decision or circumstances? What does this reveal about your desire to know and serve God better?

Why is it so important to spend at least as much time listening to God and getting to know Him as you spend telling Him things and making requests from Him?

display |

Like Jesus did, set aside some time today or tomorrow just for prayer. Choose a place to pray where you will not be interrupted. Set an alarm and don't let anything hijack your appointment with God.

During your prayer time, focus on God alone. Talk to Him—praise Him and make your requests known—but also spend time listening. Ask God questions and give Him a chance to answer or tell you what's on His mind. Write down what you think you heard God say so you can double check it in Scripture later. When Scripture verifies what we believe God tells us, we know it was Him and not from our own hearts and minds.

Thank God for the privilege of talking to Him and thank Him for choosing to talk to you. Ask God to teach you how to hear His voice and pray more effectively so you can know and represent Him better. Pray that you learn to listen closely so you don't miss a chance to play an active part in what He's doing in the world around you.

DAY 3

One Spotlight

discover |

READ MATTHEW 6:5-15.

"But when you pray, go into your private room, shut your door, and pray to your Father who is in secret. And your Father who sees in secret will reward you."
—Matthew 6:6

Times may change, but people really don't. We are just as full of ourselves today as the people in Jesus's day were—always seeking recognition, affirmation, and praise—and no one is immune, not even religious leaders.

Because the line between obeying God to show people how good He is and obeying Him to make ourselves look good is sometimes hard to discern, we must work hard to keep our motives pure so we don't steal any of God's glory by mistake. Knowing this, Jesus not only taught His disciples what to pray—words of adoration, humility, submission, dependence on God, and a desire to see Him glorified—but how to pray it as well.

Jesus knew how easy it was for people to get distracted by an audience and to start putting on a show instead of talking to God from their hearts, so He told His disciples to pray in private. Jesus also knew how easy it was for people to believe their own words were somehow responsible for the wonders God chose to perform, so He told His disciples to keep their prayers simple. Good advice!

Remember, God created us, so we can't impress Him with our words, but we can bless Him by giving Him the spotlight. Pray like it's all about Him—because it is!

delight |

How and when have you used prayer to make yourself look good?

How does the heart behind the prayers you typically pray compare to the heart behind Jesus's example prayer? What, if anything, needs to change in your prayer life?

display |

Use the template Jesus gave His disciples to write out a prayer. Begin by telling God how awesome He is—He knows, but He likes to hear it from you. Next, ask God to make everything go according to His plan—He will anyway, but asking lets you participate. Next, ask God to provide for your actual needs. Then, confess your sin and thank Him for His forgiveness. End by letting go of any grudges you've been holding and asking God to guide your steps.

As you read back over this prayer, think about how it makes God the star, not you.

> **Thank God for the privilege of prayer. Then, use the prayer you just wrote to express what's on your heart to God, but elaborate a little. Give God compliments that apply today. Ask Him to meet specific needs. Confess specific sin and tell Him who you are forgiving. Tell God where you need Him to guide your steps.**

DAY 4

More, Please, and Thank You

discover |

READ LUKE 11:5-13.

"So I say to you, ask, and it will be given to you. Seek, and you will find. Knock, and the door will be opened to you. For everyone who asks receives, and the one who seeks finds, and to the one who knocks, the door will be opened."
—Luke 11:9–10

"The squeaky wheel gets the grease," they say, and it's true. The Bible warns us not to complain, but it also tells us to bring all our prayer requests to God. Over time, as God answers with yes, no, or wait, we learn more about Him, His purposes, and how He brings them about. We get better at figuring out what He's doing and better at taking part in His plan by making requests that fall in line with His specific will for us and those around us.

One thing we know God wants for us is His Holy Spirit. The Spirit lives in everyone who has put their faith in the gospel of Jesus, of course, but He fills those who actively obey God. He teaches, guides, and empowers them and makes it possible for them to know God on a deeper level. When we ask God for more of the Spirit, He says "yes" because this request means we know Him, love Him, and want to do a better job of living for Him.

Want God's absolute best? Ask God for more of His Spirit, keep obeying, and brace yourself for awesome!

Cultivate

delight |

What do you know to be true of the Holy Spirit from your personal experience with Him?

Why might God take pleasure in granting your request for more of the Holy Spirit?

display |

Make a list of things you have recently asked God for. Next to each, record God's answers so far and what those answers have taught you about Him.

Here are a few things the Holy Spirit does for God's children: reveals sin, gives us the faith to trust God, helps us understand the Bible, empowers us to obey God, helps us pray, and helps us tell the difference between good and evil. Compare this list to your list of prayer requests and consider which is better for you in the long run—God's intervention on your behalf or more of His Spirit.

> **Thank God for being the best Father, one who knows how to give the best gifts. Thank God for listening to all of your prayer requests and giving you what you need most, even if it's not always what you want. Ask God to give you more of His Holy Spirit so you can know and serve Him better. Commit to obey Him so He can.**

DAY 5

Bring It

discover |

READ MATTHEW 5:43-48.

*"You have heard that it was said, Love your neighbor and hate your enemy.
But I tell you, love your enemies and pray for those who persecute you."*
—Matthew 5:43–44

What do you really want out of life? Your answer will determine how you pray. If what you want most is to be comfortable, prosperous, and treated right, your prayers will be mostly about your own welfare and protection. However, if what you want most is for people to see God as He is and worship Him for it, your prayers will be mostly about people coming to know God, regardless of what it costs you personally. Instead of always praying that God will punish or remove the girls who set themselves up as your enemies from your life, you'll ask God to bless them, to open their eyes to the truth, and to use you in that process.

What can you do to help? You can love the girls around you who don't deserve it. You can meet their needs like God met yours when He sent Jesus to die on the cross for your sin. This unusual behavior will draw attention, and then you can tell people about the God who loved you first and maybe introduce them to Him. Who knows? After a while, you might even welcome some adversity because it gives you a unique opportunity to glorify the Father you love!

delight |

What kinds of things do you typically ask God to do when you are being mistreated? What needs to be added to this list?

What do you think the world would be like if every Christian spent as much time praying for their enemies as they did thinking and talking about how those enemies did them wrong?

display |

In a journal or on a blank sheet of paper, list some things you have done that hurt people intentionally or accidentally. Try to remember the state of your heart and mind when you did those things. Next to each offense, identify the personal need(s) behind your actions and consider how things might have gone differently if someone had met your needs before you had a chance to speak or act. Consider the difference that loving and praying for people who hurt you could make not only in their lives, but in the lives of those around them.

Think about the girls you pictured when you read the words "love the girls around you who don't deserve it." Write out their names, and then list one practical way you can meet a need for each one of them this week—even if it's just a kind word as you pass them at school!

Thank God for loving you. Thank Him for everyone who has prayed for you and met your needs over the years. Spend time praying for the girls who have been treating you like an enemy. Ask God to show you how you can help meet their needs and then commit to follow through.

DAY 6

That's a Hard Pass

discover |

READ MATTHEW 4:1-11.

After [Jesus] had fasted forty days and forty nights, he was hungry.
—Matthew 4:2

If Adam and Eve got it wrong (and they did!), Jesus got it right. When tempted by God's enemy, Satan, to give in to the desires of the flesh and take things for Himself, Jesus turned Satan down flat. How? Well, first of all, Jesus had His priorities straight. We know from Scripture that He didn't come to serve His own glory, but God's. Adam and Eve's fall into sin showed they were really only thinking about themselves. Second, Jesus was prepared. Adam and Eve were not.

Before meeting up with Satan in the wilderness, Jesus fasted for forty days and nights. Fasting is a spiritual discipline that involves giving up something good in search of God's best, which is communion with Him. Jesus gave up food. Why? By denying Himself this basic need, Jesus communicated to God and Himself that God was not only enough for Him, but also what He wanted most.

Because the effects of physical hunger are inescapable, Jesus was constantly reminded to focus on the One for whose glory He had chosen to deny Himself. He developed perseverance and experienced God's faithfulness to sustain. By the time Satan showed up with his unimpressive offers of temporary gain, Jesus was physically weak, but more resolved than ever to play the role God had assigned Him in the advancement of His eternal kingdom.

Cultivate

delight |

Why is it important to develop perseverance and learn to rely on God before you face something that stretches you to your personal limits?

In what ways do you think fasting could help you grow in your relationship with God?

display |

Ask five girls or women who claim to know Jesus the following questions and record their answers:

Are you familiar with the spiritual discipline of fasting?

What do you understand its purpose to be?

Is there a right/wrong way to fast? Please explain.

Have you ever fasted? If not, why not? If so, what did you gain from the experience?

Consider whether you might be ready to practice fasting if you haven't ever tried it before. If you have any questions, talk with your parents or guardians, youth pastor, or small group leader.

> **Thank God for being enough and for meeting all your needs. Thank Him for speaking to your heart and for providing ways for you to know Him better. Tell God how much you love Him and want to make Him your number one priority. Tell Him about the burdens of your heart and the questions you have. Ask Him to show you whether fasting might be a way for you to understand Him and what He's doing a little better so you can join Him and resist temptation.**

"So I say to you, ask, and it will be given to you. Seek, and you will find. Knock, and the door will be opened to you. For everyone who asks receives, and the one who seeks finds, and to the one who knocks, the door will be opened."

DAY 7

Wanted: Shadow Servant

discover |

READ MATTHEW 6:16-18.

"But when you fast, put oil on your head and wash your face, so that your fasting isn't obvious to others but to your Father who is in secret. And your Father who sees in secret will reward you."
—Matthew 6:17–18

Why do God's children fast? For the same reason they do everything else: to glorify God and to show the world who He is and what He has done so people will give Him the praise and recognition He deserves. To do the best job of this, we have to hear what He says and learn to rely on Him. The problem is, we live in a noisy world full of people, things, pursuits, and ideas that compete for our attention and affection. If we don't stop once in a while and make ourselves focus on God alone, we could miss out on hearing something important.

That's where fasting comes in. Fasting is giving up something good in search of God's best. When we give up something that leaves a void, the pain, discomfort, or inconvenience caused by that void drives us to God, teaches us to rely on Him, and develops perseverance in us as we listen for His voice. However, it's only effective if we do it privately. When we make a show of going without, we tempt ourselves to focus more on how people respond to us than on what God is saying. Doing this draws the attention of others away from God and to ourselves. When we do this, we defeat the whole purpose.

Want to glorify God? Stay in His shadow. Always.

delight

What do people tend to think of those who make a big deal of their own spiritual obedience? How does this undermine their efforts?

What do you want or need from God right now? What are you willing to give up to understand what He's thinking on the matter?

display |

If you're ready to practice fasting, give something up (like video games or TikTok®) for a few days or a week for the purpose of discovering God's best for you in a specific area of concern. Choose something that will leave a void big enough to remind you to focus on God, but not cause you harm. When you are drawn to do that activity you gave up, be reminded to focus on God, pray, and listen for His voice. Jot down everything you learn from the experience.

Tell God what you love about Him. Let Him know you understand that everything good in your life is from Him. Ask God to use you to get the glory He deserves for all this. Commit to redirect any praise or recognition you get to Him from now on.

DAY 8

Don't Wait

discover |

READ LUKE 2:41-50.

And all those who heard [Jesus] were astounded
at his understanding and his answers.
—Luke 2:47

You can watch all the makeup tutorials and tips videos available on TikTok®, but doing so won't magically apply the makeup to your own face on prom night. And you wouldn't expect it to! After watching several times, you'd probably buy some of the products they recommend, then you'd likely try the look at home a few times to get it just right before trying it out in public.

If you only crack open your Bible when someone else is teaching it, it'll take you a while to know, understand, and talk about the Bible with confidence. Preachers, Bible teachers, and mentors are great, but we can study the Bible on our own as well. The same Holy Spirit who lives in them lives in you, too! The Bible says He helps us understand and apply the Bible to our individual lives. Of course, He can't help us with something we aren't actively doing, so we have to get in there—read, study, meditate, and memorize—and give Him something to work with.

Jesus didn't wait. Before He was even old enough to join your student ministry, Jesus studied the Bible and talked about it with all kinds of people—even temple teachers. Whether He was actually learning from them or just helping them along in their thinking, we don't know, but we do know it was His idea. He didn't need pushing; neither should we!

Cultivate

delight |

How would you describe your personal Bible study habits? Use these journalistic questions to answer.

Who do I study the Bible with?

What helps me study the Bible?

When do I study the Bible?

Where do I study the Bible?

Why do I study the Bible?

How do I study the Bible?

display |

Make a list of spiritual questions you have. Ask several girls or women whose lives prove they know and obey the Bible what passages you should read to find answers. Don't let them give you the answer; find it yourself with the Holy Spirit's help, then check back with them to see if they came to the same conclusion. If you still have questions, go ahead and ask them what they believe about those things and why. Ask them to show you Bible verses that back up their opinion.

Thank God for the Bible and for giving you the Holy Spirit to help you understand and apply it. Ask God to reveal His truth to you as you make the effort to read, study, memorize, and meditate on His Word.

DAY 9

Get Out There

discover |

READ LUKE 4:16-30.

[Jesus] came to Nazareth, where he had been brought up. As usual, he
entered the synagogue on the Sabbath day and stood up to read.
—Luke 4:16

Have you ever worried that you don't know enough to make a difference in the world? Don't. God doesn't choose the equipped; He equips the chosen. All you have to do is study your Bible and rely on God to use it for His glory. That's what Jesus did.

Jesus was the Messiah, the One sent and chosen by God to rescue the entire world from the consequences of sin. But He wasn't born knowing everything He would need to know to do the job. Like the rest of us, Jesus had to go to the synagogue (something similar to church for us today) and study on His own to learn all He needed to know. As He did, God rewarded His efforts with knowledge and wisdom. By the time Jesus began His ministry, He knew the Word well enough to resist the devil, who tried to twist Scripture around, and apply biblical truth to what was going on around Him—from memory!

People didn't always like what Jesus had to say, but He never second-guessed His convictions or changed His message to make them happy. Confident because He knew God's Word for Himself, Jesus kept preaching the truth, and God kept protecting Him as He obeyed. He'll do the same for you! Study up and get out there!

delight |

On a scale from one to ten, how confident are you in your ability to explain to others what the Bible says or to tell them how it applies to what they are going through?

1	2	3	4	5	6	7	8	9	10
Don't look at me					Eh, sort of			I've got this	

Why is it so important for children of God to know what the Bible says for themselves instead of relying on other people to tell them?

Why is it so important to study the Bible for yourself before you start trying to tell others what it says?

display |

Name several current hot-button topics. Circle those you have taken the time to look up in the Bible for yourself. Put a star next to the circled topics you have also thought about prayerfully in relationship to current events. These are the only ones you might be qualified to give an opinion on when you have been obeying God consistently and can hear the Holy Spirit clearly.

Use your list to make a to-do prayer/study list. Take the first step(s) today.

Thank God for giving you His Word so you can know Him better. Ask God to help you understand what you are reading when you study it. Ask Him to give you wisdom and discernment as you try to figure out how it relates to what's going on in the world around you. Commit to doing the work so you can represent Him well like Jesus did.

DAY 10

Boss Bible

discover |

READ MATTHEW 22:23-33.

*Jesus answered them, "You are mistaken, because you
don't know the Scriptures or the power of God."*
—Matthew 22:29

It's possible to know just enough of your Bible to be dangerous. The
Sadducees in today's reading are one example. Hoping to trip Jesus
up and embarrass Him so people wouldn't follow Him anymore, they
tried to use God's Word against Him. The problem was, Jesus knew
Scripture better than they did. The question they asked wasn't even a
good question because the situation they described couldn't happen—
something they would have known if they had studied God's Word as a
whole instead of tearing off pieces to serve their own purposes.

The Bible helps us know God better, but it's more than a tool. It's the
ultimate authority on all matters. Because its application is so broad, it
must be studied as a whole. When we clip out and save in our mental
scrapbooks only what we like or think might serve us at some point, we
run the risk of misinterpreting the Bible and misleading others.

Want to make sure you're being a help to God and not hindering His
plan? Study the Bible, but don't try to master it. Stay teachable and let it
master you!

delight |

What's wrong with using Bible verses to serve your own purposes?

What are some things you can do to make sure people are not using the Bible to manipulate you for their own purposes?

display |

Here are some popular Bible verses people like to quote: Psalm 46:5;
Jeremiah 29:11; Luke 11:9; Romans 8:28; 1 Corinthians 10:13;
Philippians 4:13; and 1 Timothy 6:10. For each, write how/when people
like to use these verses.

Psalm 46:5

Jeremiah 29:11

Luke 11:9

Romans 8:28

1 Corinthians 10:13

Philippians 4:13

1 Timothy 6:10

Choose one of the verses in this list to look up and read in context (with
the rest of the verses in the section or chapter). Does reading the verse
in context change how people tend to use it? How it might be better
used based on its context within Scripture?

Thank God for giving you His Word, the Bible, to read and obey
so you can know and serve Him better. Ask Him to correct you by
whatever means necessary when you're tempted to use the Bible
to serve your own purposes. Commit to studying the Bible for
yourself so you can tell when people are trying to mislead you.

SECTION 2

Outward Disciplines

When Jesus sets a girl free on the inside, it shows up on the outside. Over time, she stops craving wealth, fame, power, and success like everyone else does. Instead, she finds joy and contentment in simplicity, solitude with God, submission, and service like Jesus did because it brings her closer to the One who matters most—the Father.

DAY 11

Eyes Up

discover |

READ LUKE 9:57-62.

Jesus told him, "Foxes have dens, and birds of the sky have nests, but the Son of Man has no place to lay his head."
—Luke 9:58

Some of us are less committed to following Jesus than we think we are. Sure, we are willing to go without some possessions, comfort, relationships, safety, and so on, but we secretly hope God never asks us to give up everything like Jesus did.

The first man in today's reading was feeling pretty good about what he'd endured so far, so he made a radical promise similar to the kind many of us make. When Jesus reminded the man that following Him could mean homelessness, the man didn't even respond. Then Jesus called someone else to follow, but that man wanted to wait a while before leaving to make sure he would have a home and living to come back to later. Jesus reminded him that serving God's eternal kingdom was more important than securing any temporary estate.

The man who then volunteered wasn't very concerned about his estate, but he did want to take steps to preserve family relationships before leaving. In response, Jesus made it very clear we can't let anything or anyone distract or delay us from obeying Jesus. The truth is, if you belong to God, this world isn't your home—and this is good because, sooner or later, it will all be gone. Your home is heaven. Stay focused and live simply!

delight |

What have you sacrificed to follow Jesus so far? What are you afraid God might ask you to give up in the future?

What kinds of excuses do people offer God when He asks them to make His kingdom their number one priority?

display |

The discipline we'll explore over the next three days is simplicity. Take a few minutes to consider all the things girls you know have given up to serve God's kingdom. Make a list. Next to each girl's sacrifice, write about the positive impact it has had on you. Text, call, or send a note to one of these girls. On behalf of God's family, thank them for their sacrifice (be as specific as possible) and then tell them how their sacrifice has influenced you personally.

Thank God for the gift of His Son Jesus and for all the sacrifices Jesus made even before He died on the cross. Thank God for the privilege of serving His kingdom like Jesus did and ask Him to stir in your heart a desire to see Him glorified that far outweighs your desire for anything else. Thank God for heaven and ask Him to give you a longing for it.

DAY 12

Let Go Already

discover |

READ MARK 10:17-31.

Looking at him, Jesus loved him and said to him, "You lack one thing: Go, sell all you have and give to the poor, and you will have treasure in heaven. Then come, follow me."
—Mark 10:21

How much stuff do you own? Do you have the latest fashion trends? Top of the line products? The newest smartphone? Are you sure? It probably seemed to those around him like the rich young man in today's reading had everything, but he didn't. Something was missing, and he knew it. That's why he came to Jesus.

What the young man lacked was freedom. In truth, he didn't really own his possessions; they owned him and were keeping him from experiencing true joy. He cared too much about what he had and believed too much in his own ability to earn everything he needed for himself—even his salvation—to let himself believe Jesus could be enough. Knowing this, Jesus told the man to sell everything. If he had, it would have been an outward expression of inner surrender to God through faith in Jesus Christ, and the young man would have found the freedom he craved.

Jesus doesn't ask all of us to sell everything we have to follow Him, but He does call us to salvation through faith. This salvation requires surrender, so we must learn to hold loosely anything we may be tempted to call our own. Everything we think we have actually belongs to God, and He has every right to make our lives simpler by taking it back.

delight |

In what ways are you held captive by the things you own?

Why is it so hard to rely fully on God instead of yourself?

display

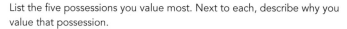

List the five possessions you value most. Next to each, describe why you value that possession.

Now think through a typical day. Explain what you do on a regular basis to take care of or enjoy those things. Next to each, record the amount of time required.

Compare the amount of time and effort you put into maintaining and enjoying your possessions to the amount of time and effort you put into maintaining your relationship with Jesus and enjoying Him.

What changes might you need to make?

> **Thank God for blessing you with resources you can invest in His kingdom. Ask Him to forgive you for the times you have allowed your possessions to keep you from knowing and serving Him like He wants. Tell God everything you have is His. If/when you mean it, commit to live in a state of constant surrender to His will, no matter the cost.**

DAY 13

Smash Those Idols

discover |

READ MATTHEW 6:19-24.

"For where your treasure is, there your heart will be also."
—Matthew 6:21

Could you have been taken prisoner without realizing it? Maybe. Sometimes, the ropes that bind us are invisible. Sometimes, we tie the knots ourselves—not on purpose of course, but it's possible to do right things the wrong way or for the wrong reason and fall into sin. Jesus knew this and warned against it.

God expects us to develop and invest what He's given us—resources, relationships, talents and abilities, spiritual gifts, and our freedom in Christ—but we must be careful to develop and invest those things according to His will. Remember, God's ultimate purpose in all things is His glory, so we have to make sure our goal is always to show the world who He is and what He's done so He can get the praise and recognition He deserves. When we make the development of what He's given us our number one priority, we turn these blessings into idols, and when we use these things to please or bring attention to ourselves, we become our own idols. Either way, we enslave ourselves to sin.

Bottom line: we love what we serve. Want to walk in the freedom Jesus died to give you? Keep it simple. Serve God and His purposes only. Pay close attention not only to what you do, but also why and how you do it. Smash those idols and make sure they stay smashed!

delight |

When have you turned a God-given gift into an idol?

Why is this so easy to do?

display |

Practice the discipline of simplicity today or tomorrow. Go into your room and see what you have that you either don't need anymore, don't use anymore, or don't want anymore. It could be nice clothes you don't wear anymore or shoes, purses, sunglasses, books, and even makeup that's been left unopened. Make sure it's okay with your parents first, then take those unused items to a ministry or place in your community where people could use them. Don't sell them or try to profit in any way; just give away these things, knowing that letting someone have them that can use them is sure better than them sitting in your house collecting dust.

Thank God for the opportunity to love and serve Him. Tell Him all the reasons He deserves to be recognized and praised. Ask Him to get your attention by any means necessary when you start to worship anything or anyone but Him. Commit to using everything He's given you to worship Him as He deserves.

DAY 14

Beyond Good

discover |

READ LUKE 6:12-16.

During those days [Jesus] went out to the mountain
to pray and spent all night in prayer to God.
—Luke 6:12

Sometimes life gets so loud it's hard to hear yourself think, much less discern God's voice. This was certainly true for Jesus. Between the people who wanted to trip Him up, the people who wanted to exploit Him, and the people who loved Him but didn't quite understand God's will, Jesus was surrounded by misguided people. No doubt, many of them would have been happy to advise Jesus, but the only opinion that mattered to Him was God's.

In this passage, Jesus spent all night alone with God before picking His twelve disciples—a choice that had a big impact on His ministry. Although some might argue that Jesus didn't really need to lose sleep over it and that any of Jesus's many disciples would have done at least as well as Judas Iscariot given the chance, Jesus knew God's way was always best. So, He shut out the world to make sure He knew what God's way was.

Until we learn to do the same, we run the risk of mishearing God's instruction. Then, when difficulty comes like it did for Jesus with Judas, we won't know whether the challenge we're facing is part of God's plan or a consequence of disobedience. In so many ways, solitude with God brings peace. Alone time with God isn't just good; it's vital!

Cultivate

delight |

Why is it a bad idea to make big decisions without spending a significant amount of time in two-way conversation with God?

What should you do when the advice a person gives you goes against what you think God is telling you to do?

display |

Over the next three days, we'll explore the discipline of solitude. Jot down some decisions you will need to make soon and/or things that have been on your mind lately. Schedule some time alone with God—no people, no social media, no music, no anything. Tell God about everything on your list and ask Him to give you His opinion. Work through your list slowly, giving God time to answer. Focus as He brings feelings, memories, Scripture, circumstances, people, and so on to mind, and write out what you think you hear. When you are finished, circle anything you wrote that can be backed up with Scripture. Pay attention to these!

Thank God for wanting to spend time alone with you, speak to you, and guide you. Ask Him to help you discern His voice as you practice solitude. Ask for the wisdom to make good decisions and the faith to act on what He says instead of on what other people say. Commit to doing what He tells you to do so you don't have any regrets.

DAY 15

Right Now vs. Forever

discover |

READ MATTHEW 14:13-14.

When Jesus heard about [John the Baptist's death], he withdrew from there by boat to a remote place to be alone. When the crowds heard this, they followed him on foot from the towns. When he went ashore, he saw a large crowd, had compassion on them, and healed their sick.
—Matthew 14:13-14

When Jesus found out that His cousin, John the Baptist, had been beheaded, Jesus did what most modern professionals would have advised Him to do: He tried to get a little space to process and heal. Knowing Jesus's habits like we do, we can assume He planned to process and heal with His heavenly Father, but the crowds didn't let Him.

Jesus could have sent the crowds away, and no one would have blamed Him—it could be argued that He would have been practicing good stewardship of Himself—but Jesus was able to zoom out, see things from God's perspective, and make the better choice. Jesus was suffering, but so were the people. If He had sent them away, some who ended up putting their faith in Him might not have.

When life gets hard, it's difficult to think past the here and now, but every decision is an eternal decision. Definitely take good care of yourself so you can keep serving God's kingdom well, but remember that the spiritual needs of eternal souls always outweigh the needs of temporary bodies. Like Jesus did, do your best to meet the second as it best serves the first. With the Holy Spirit's help, find balance.

delight |

How do you usually decide whether to see to other girls' needs or your own in a given moment?

How do appropriate personal sacrifices made by God's children help Him get the glory He deserves?

display |

Describe some times recently when you have put your own needs before the needs of others. Cross out the times you couldn't have found a way to meet the needs of others and still be a good steward of your own God-given self. Next, note a few times you have put the needs of others before your own recently. Compare lists and consider the pattern of behavior they reveal.

Thank God for meeting your every need according to His riches. Thank Him for giving you an eternal purpose and ask Him to remind you of that purpose when you forget. Ask Him to help you make wise choices when you have to choose between meeting your own needs and meeting the needs of others.

DAY 16

Go Against the Flow

discover |

READ JOHN 6:1-15.

Therefore, when Jesus realized that they were about to come and take him by force to make him king, he withdrew again to the mountain by himself.
—John 6:15

Do you ever get swept up in a moment or carried away by emotion? It's easy to do. That's why Jesus guarded against it. After He fed the five thousand, the people whose needs Jesus had just met wanted to make Him king. They didn't want Him as king because they believed it was God's plan, but because they thought having a guy like Jesus as king would benefit them. Had Jesus allowed it, He would have been stepping outside of God's plan and accepting less than the title God had already given Him: King of kings.

Human logic might argue that Jesus allowing the people to make Him king would have helped Him get His gospel message across and offered Him a measure of protection, but it would have undermined His mission. Jesus's job was to proclaim the truth and serve as the sacrifice for our sins. If He had the protection of a human title, Jesus might not have been crucified—something that was absolutely necessary.

To keep from being swept up in the political current and, maybe, to resist temptation similar to what He had experienced in the wilderness alone with Satan, Jesus got alone with God. When we practice solitude like Jesus, our spirit is renewed, our perspective restored, and we stay on the right path.

Cultivate

delight |

When have you been swept up in a moment or gotten carried away by emotion and stepped outside of God's plan? How might solitude with God have helped you?

Why is it so important to do what God tells you to do rather than give in to others' desires?

display |

Practice solitude today or tomorrow. Even if it's only for a short time, find a way to get alone with God. Maybe if you're old enough to drive, take a drive out to a quiet place and just be alone with the Lord. If you can't drive yet, go to your room or another quiet place in your neighborhood and just sit in silence for a while. Eliminate all distractions. Take your Bible, a notebook, and a pen, and just sit quietly. A word of warning: It may feel awkward at first, but press through the awkwardness and remain in the silence. Try to focus your mind on God and God alone. Explore the Scriptures in front of you. Write in your notebook what you feel and how you hear Him speaking to you. Enjoy the silence. Enjoy time alone with God.

Thank God for being faithful to guide you in the decisions you make. Thank Him for renewing your strength when you feel weak and for helping you recognize and resist temptation when you listen for His voice. Commit to getting alone with Him and asking what He wants you to do instead of rushing ahead and doing what people want you to do.

_____

Jesus called them over and said to them, "You know that those who are regarded as rulers of the Gentiles lord it over them, and those in high positions act as tyrants over them. But it is not so among you. On the contrary, whoever wants to become great among you will be your servant, and whoever wants to be first among you will be a slave to all. For even the Son of Man did not come to be served, but to serve, and to give his life as a ransom for many."

DAY 17

Winners Submit

discover |

READ MATTHEW 5:38-42.

"And if anyone forces you to go one mile, go with him two."
—Matthew 5:41

When someone submits in a wrestling match, that means they lose the match. When a group of dogs who haven't ever been around each other get together, they often scrap and wrestle with each other until they all submit to the alpha dog. Submission implies giving up. It is a word most people don't like.

Then why did Jesus teach His followers to submit to others? In today's passage, He explained that when a soldier forces you to walk one mile, you should submit to him and willingly go another. This seems counterintuitive. However, when you remember that our job as God's children is to show the world who He is and tell them what He's done, it makes more sense.

God is love. He extends grace by treating people better than they deserve to be treated. He shows mercy by showing compassionate restraint when dealing with people who have done wrong. Jesus demonstrated these truths by submitting on the cross. This is the gospel. We can tell it all we want, but until we prove and illustrate it by submitting to others according to God's will, people won't believe it's true or understand this gospel is for them.

It's hard to respond to hate in love, but when we do it for the sake of the gospel, God's kingdom grows, He is glorified, and we all win.

delight |

What is your typical response when people aren't kind to you? What does this response tell people about your heavenly Father?

Although God calls us to serve others, He expects us to obey Him in all things. How should you respond when someone asks you to do something that goes against God's Word?

display |

The next two days will explore the discipline of submission. Let's be honest: it's not easy to submit to others. Write your future self a note of encouragement today. Read this note and reflect on what it means to submit to others. Submission that leads us or others to sin is not what God is after. Submission that reveals the love of God and displays the truth of the gospel is why God calls us to submit. Let that drive your thoughts as you encourage yourself to submit to others.

Thank God for showing you grace and mercy through Jesus and for the opportunity to show that same grace and mercy to the girls around you. Ask God to give you strength as you submit to those who do not love you the way you try to love them. Thank God for the privilege of representing Jesus even when it's not easy.

DAY 18

Making it Count

discover |

READ MATTHEW 26:36-44.

Going a little farther, [Jesus] fell facedown and prayed, "My Father, if it is possible, let this cup pass from me. Yet not as I will, but as you will."
—Matthew 26:39

We know Jesus died on the cross to set us free from sin, but what made Him do it? What in the world compelled Jesus to let people beat Him and nail Him to a tree? We'd like to think it was love for us, but Jesus's struggle in the Garden of Gethsemane the night before His arrest suggests otherwise. Oh, Jesus loves us—there's no doubt—but when it came right down to it, Jesus died on the cross because God told Him to. Jesus loved God. More than anything else, Jesus wanted God to get the praise and recognition He deserved for being who He is and for doing all He's done, so He submitted to God's plan and trusted God to make His obedience count for His glory.

Mustering up affection for God is easy, but loving Him with our lives is not. It often requires us to make sacrifices we'd rather not make. However, if we truly love God and want to see Him glorified as He deserves, we will submit like Jesus did. Even when it's hard, even when we have doubts, even when we wish there could be another way, we will obey God and trust Him to know best and make our sacrifices count.

Cultivate

delight |

What's wrong with trying to do what God asks you to do the way you want to do it versus how He wants you to do it?

What did God's willingness to sacrifice His beloved, sinless Son for us tell the world about Him? His love for people?

display |

Ask a woman who obviously loves Jesus about the sacrifices God has asked her to make for His glory. Start by asking her to tell you about a sacrifice she made and how God used that sacrifice. Then, ask her to tell you about a sacrifice she didn't make and to share her thoughts and feelings about that decision now. Thank her for her honesty. Summarize her testimony and keep it to read and encourage you when God asks you to make sacrifices in the future.

Thank God for sending Jesus to pay the price for your sin so you could call Him Father. Tell Him how important it is to you for Him to get the glory He deserves. Commit to making the sacrifices He asks you to make even when they don't make sense to you. Thank Him for always making your obedience count.

DAY 19

Great Service

discover |

READ MARK 10:35-45.

"But it is not so among you. On the contrary, whoever wants
to become great among you will be your servant, and whoever
wants to be first among you will be a slave to all."
—*Mark 10:43–44*

Have you ever gone to a restaurant and been greeted with a warm smile, seated promptly at a clean table, served by cheerful staff, and brought delicious food quicker than you expected? When this happens, you're not only likely to return, you're likely to recommend the restaurant to others.

Service is critical for restaurants and for Christ-followers. In today's Scripture passage, Jesus laid out His expectation for people who follow Him: we are to be servants. This flips the normal thought process of the world upside down. Most say, "To be first, you have to elbow your way to the front of the line." Jesus said the opposite.

When we take on the task of being a servant, we not only live opposite of the world, but we also live in a way that is appealing to others. Being a servant is not always celebrated, but it glorifies the Father and reveals the Spirit's work inside of us.

Service is a spiritual discipline. It doesn't come naturally. It's something we have to work on and something God has to do in us. When we're willing to learn to serve like Jesus did, greatness awaits us. To be great in the eyes of God, we have to be like that extraordinary restaurant— willing to serve.

delight |

How could being willing to serve others draw people to Jesus?

When have you been well served by another believer? How can you apply the lesson they showed you with their service to others?

display |

Make a list of women who are well known or hold a position of authority because of their relationship with Jesus. For each, name one way God is using that woman to advance His kingdom. Next, name one way each person could abuse the fame or power God has given them and the negative consequences that could result. Consider your own readiness to handle the kind of responsibility each of these people carry.

Thank God for the privilege of knowing Him and for letting you help advance His kingdom. Thank God for knowing just how much responsibility to give you right now. Commit to using it to serve Him, not yourself. Pray for each of the people on the list you just made. Ask God to keep them strong and to help them continue to make wise choices for His sake.

DAY 20

Loving the Bad Guys

discover |

READ JOHN 13:1-17.

So [Jesus] got up from supper, laid aside his outer clothing, took a towel, and tied it around himself. Next, he poured water into a basin and began to wash his disciples' feet and to dry them with the towel wrapped around him.
—John 13:4-5

It's hard to love people who aren't loving you back, but that doesn't excuse you from doing it.

Jesus was a man, but He was also God. He knew Judas Iscariot would betray Him before He ever asked Judas to become a disciple. Even so, Jesus took care of Judas and invested in him. Jesus treated Judas just as well as the apostles who would eventually be martyred for remaining faithful to Him. He even washed Judas's feet the night Judas handed Him over to be killed in exchange for money! Why? God told Him to. In serving Judas, Jesus painted a beautiful picture of God's love for us, which is neither earned nor conditional, but a constant outflow of His character aimed our direction.

When we serve those who wouldn't serve us, we illustrate the gospel of Jesus, who died for all people—even those who refuse to love Him back. You can't control how people treat you, but you can control the way you treat them. When you're tempted to withhold love from someone, do what Jesus did. For the sake of God's glory, take up the towel and serve, even if they don't appreciate it.

Cultivate

delight |

When have you been guilty of deciding for yourself whom you will serve and whom you will not?

When have you received love you didn't deserve?

display |

Make a list of girls you don't feel like serving at the moment. Go back through your list and circle the names of the girls you are likely to interact with today. Next to each name, write down one thing you can do to serve and encourage them. Do these things and/or anything else God tells you to do when you interact with them. At the end of the day, write down your experiences, what you did, how they responded, who was blessed, and what God taught you.

Thank God for knowing what you think and how you act and loving you anyway. Thank God for Jesus's willingness to serve you on the cross out of love for Him. Ask God to help you see people through His eyes. Commit to serving others when you get the chance for His sake even when they don't deserve it.

SECTION 3

Corporate Disciplines

Some spiritual disciplines we do alone. Others we do with others. Corporate disciplines are ones we do with other believers. When we put our faith in the gospel of Jesus for salvation, we not only become God's child but also members of an eternal family. Bound by the Holy Spirit, brothers and sisters in Jesus are responsible to and for one another. When we cooperate through worship, stewardship, and fellowship for God's glory, everyone is blessed.

DAY 21

Him Only

discover |

READ LUKE 4:1-13.

And Jesus answered him, "It is written: Worship
the Lord your God, and serve him only."
—Luke 4:8

To worship someone or something is to use what you have to honor that person or thing. The devil tried to tempt Jesus to worship him, but it would have been a really foolish trade if Jesus had given in. The devil only offered Jesus authority over earthly kingdoms, but God had already given Jesus all authority in heaven and on earth. Had Jesus used what God had given Him to honor the devil, He would have received less in return than what He already had.

The same is true for us. The devil may offer us all kinds of things in return for our worship, but we are foolish if we give it. As children of God, those of us who have put our faith in Jesus for salvation are co-heirs of God's kingdom with Jesus Himself. Nothing is impossible for us because nothing is impossible for our heavenly Father. Holy, all-powerful, all-knowing, endless, unchanging, and so on, God alone is worthy of our worship—both private and corporate (with our brothers and sisters).

Even if we give God all we have, we benefit far more than He does from the transaction. Make no mistake; worshiping God is always the right and best thing to do!

delight |

What or whom have you been guilty of worshiping besides God, intentionally or unintentionally? What steps led you to giving so much affection to something or someone other than God?

In what ways do you use what God has given you to worship Him?

display |

For the next three days, we'll focus on the spiritual discipline of worship. Take some time to worship God today. There are many ways to worship Him—listen to a playlist of hymns or praise music, sing or play music yourself, enjoy the world He created by taking a walk in nature, or even create your own work of art. No matter how you spend your time worshiping Him, make sure that He is 100 percent the focus. As you worship, visualize Jesus and lift your heart in praise and worship to Him.

Thank God for being a generous, loving God and for always giving you more than you give Him. Thank God for providing you with resources you can use to honor Him. Thank God for brothers and sisters with whom you can worship. Ask God to show you how to cooperate with them to bring Him the most glory.

DAY 22

As He Intended

discover |

READ MARK 2:23-28.

Then [Jesus] told them, "The Sabbath was made for man and not man
for the Sabbath. So then, the Son of Man is Lord even of the Sabbath."
—Mark 2:27-28

Following the instruction in God's Word is good because it shows us
who He is, reveals our need for Him, guides us in righteous living, and
teaches us how to represent Him to the rest of the world. However,
it's easy for us to forget why God gave us instructions in His Word. If
we aren't careful, we can start worshiping God's laws instead of God
Himself—something Jesus warned against.

When Jesus and His disciples did what the Pharisees considered unlawful
on the Sabbath, Jesus had to set them straight. God didn't create the
Sabbath so we could be bound by lists of rules on how to honor God
correctly. Instead, He created the Sabbath so we could worship God
and rest. He made it to give us a time to focus our hearts on God and to
recharge our batteries to better serve Him throughout the week.

When the Pharisees objected, Jesus called Himself "Lord of the
Sabbath," asserting His right to decide what was and was not the proper
way to worship God. He is God, after all. We don't have the same right
to decide, but if we follow Jesus's lead and use each Sabbath day to
worship God, rest, and focus our hearts on Him, we are honoring the
Sabbath as He intended.

Cultivate

delight |

What has God's law taught you about Him and your need for Him?

Are you honoring the Sabbath each week? Rate yourself on a scale of one to ten on how you are honoring the God through the Sabbath. How can you improve in using the Sabbath in the way God intented for it to be used?

display |

While you don't have to make every Sunday the Sabbath, you do need to take a day each week to worship God and rest. Whether it's the next Sunday or another day when you have opportunity, within the next seven days, take a Sabbath day. Make the focus of that day worship and rest. Write out a plan for how you can spend your next Sabbath day worshiping God and resting.

Thank God for giving you the Sabbath day. Acknowledge that sometimes we try to make it about things other than Him. Ask Him to remind you that Sabbath is about spending time focusing your heart on Him through worship and recharging your internal batteries through rest.

DAY 23

First Things First

discover |
READ MATTHEW 21:12-13.

*Jesus went into the temple and threw out all those buying and selling.
He overturned the tables of the money changers and the chairs of
those selling doves. He said to them, "It is written, My house will be
called a house of prayer, but you are making it a den of thieves!"*
—Matthew 21:12-13

More than anything else, Jesus wanted to see God glorified for being
who He is and for doing what He's done. Everything Jesus ever said
or did served this purpose, including His participation in organized
corporate worship. In fact, the only thing that ever really frustrated Jesus
or made Him angry was when something or someone got in the way of
God being worshiped properly.

When Jesus entered Jerusalem for the last time, He turned the temple
courtyard upside down—not because people were selling animals and
exchanging coins (these practices were necessary for some people to
present the sacrifices God had asked them to present), but because the
system had become corrupt. The priests were actually turning a profit
from selling items they knew the people had to have to participate in
worship. What's more, the market had been set up in the only part of
the temple where Gentiles were allowed, interfering with their ability to
worship God.

This was unacceptable to Jesus. He had come to rid the world of sin
and make communion with God possible, so He began by cleansing the
temple. If we're smart, we'll let Him do the same in us!

delight |

In what ways do we take worship and turn it into something it's not supposed to be? Why is this dangerous for the person doing it?

What can you do to help focus on the true point of worship—glorifying God—in your own heart?

display |

Jump in a time machine today! Not literally, but search the song by Matt Redman called "Heart of Worship" on a music streaming platform or in a search engine. Listen to the song and read the lyrics. Consider if there are ways you've made worship something God didn't intend it to be. Repent where necessary and come back to the heart of worship in your own life. It's all about Him!

Thank God for making it possible for you to know Him through Jesus. Thank Him for welcoming you into His presence. Thank Him for a church family to worship with. Confess the times you have gotten in the way of someone who was trying to know Him better or worship Him and commit to being a helper in that process from now on.

DAY 24

How Much Is "Enough"?

discover |

READ MATTHEW 6:25-34.

"And why do you worry about clothes? Observe how the wildflowers of the field grow; They don't labor or spin thread. Yet I tell you that not even Solomon in all of his splendor was adorned like one of these. If that's how God clothes the grass of the filed, which is here today and thrown into the furnace tomorrow, won't he do much more for you—you of little faith?"
—*Matthew 6:28-30*

How much do you really need? That's a hard question to answer. Jesus told His disciples God would provide for all their needs, but then only listed food and clothing. Jesus knew the disciples would never be rich, so He didn't tell them they would be. Instead, He called their attention to God's ongoing provision for His creation and the obvious beauty all around them.

If they wanted to follow God faithfully, Jesus's disciples couldn't let themselves get caught up in the quest for material gain. They needed to change the way they thought and learn how to differentiate between wants and needs. If they didn't, they would never be satisfied with what they had.

If you have put your faith in the gospel of Jesus, you are not just God's creation—you are His child, and He will provide for you. Don't get hung up on what you don't have. If you don't have it, you probably don't need it, and if you do need it, it's coming. Just keep giving everything back to God, and He will keep providing. It's all His anyway!

Cultivate

delight |

What is the difference between a want and a need? Why do we get the two confused sometimes?

Does the way you think about, talk about, pursue, and display worldly goods tell the world that your relationship with God is enough? Explain.

display |

For the next three days, we'll explore the spiritual discipline of stewardship, which means caring for what we've been given. Write God a traditional thank you letter. In this letter, thank Him for what you have. Include your possessions, resources, relationships, and opportunities. Thank Him for providing for all your needs and for some of your wants. Thank Him for what He's done for you, beginning with Jesus. Tell God what you plan to do with what He's given you and end by thanking Him again for His generosity.

Thank God for loving you and providing for all your needs. If you are guilty of any greed or idolatry, confess it and accept His forgiveness. Ask God to teach you the difference between wants and needs. Commit to being content with whatever He chooses to give you and to use it for His glory.

Matthew 6:28-30

"And why do you worry about clothes? Observe how the wildflowers of the field grow; They don't labor or spin thread. Yet I tell you that not even Solomon in all of his splendor was adorned like one of these. If that's how God clothes the grass of the field, which is here today and thrown into the furnace tomorrow, won't He do much more for you—you of little faith?"

DAY 25

Don't Miss Out

discover |

READ MARK 12:13-17.

Jesus told them, "Give to Caesar the things that are Caesar's, and to God
the things that are God's." And they were utterly amazed at him.
—Mark 12:17

The fact that the religious rulers of Jesus's day thought they could trick Him proves just how arrogant and ignorant they were. In today's reading, they were looking for an excuse to arrest Jesus, so they tried to get Him to say something that would upset the government authorities. They thought Jesus would say that the people shouldn't pay taxes, but He didn't. Instead, Jesus encouraged them to be good stewards, or caretakers, of what God had allowed them to have.

Contrary to what the religious leaders believed, the question of taxes wasn't about showing loyalty to God or country, but showing loyalty to God by obeying the powers in place simply because God had allowed them to rule, thereby showing faith in His wisdom.

Everything belongs to God. He just lets us hold it for a while. We honor Him and participate in His plan when we invest the money He lets us hold in a manner consistent with His will and character. That means before you spend, be sure to consider what God would have you do with His money. Don't put it in the wrong place and miss a chance to glorify Him!

delight |

How should the fact that everything in the world is God's impact the way you handle money?

How would the world be different if everyone tried to honor God with their money?

display |

Think about the money you have right now at this stage in your life. It might not be very much, but the Bible teaches that when we are faithful with small things, God will trust us with bigger things (see Matt. 25:21). This is in no way to say that if you are faithful to God with small amounts of money, He'll be forced to give you large amounts of money. What it means is that when you desire to be faithful with whatever you have, it builds a habit in you and reveals that God can begin to trust you as He gives you more in the future.

Are you in the practice of tithing, or giving God back 10 percent of the money you make? Today, with whatever money you have—whether from a job, allowance, birthday, or a good report card—figure out how much 10 percent is. Then pray about how you should give that money back to God. It might mean putting it in the offering plate on Sunday. It might mean that you donate it to a local ministry that serves people in your community. However you feel led to give, begin the practice now of giving God back 10 percent of what He's entrusted you with.

Thank God for trusting you to take care of some of what belongs to Him. Ask Him to teach you how to give and share as generously as He does. Confess any mishandling of His possessions and commit to hold what some people might consider to be yours loosely so you won't be tempted to mishandle His possessions again.

DAY 26

Always Enough

discover |

READ LUKE 9:10-17.

Everyone ate and was filled. They picked up twelve baskets of leftover pieces.
—Luke 9:17

In today's reading, the disciples didn't think they had enough resources to provide for the crowd that followed Jesus. In fact, the idea of feeding them seemed so impossible the disciples didn't even consider trying. Instead, they asked Jesus to send the people away so they could get what they needed for themselves—but Jesus had other plans.

Jesus was so secure in God's provision that He told the disciples to feed the people with what didn't even look like it would be enough to feed them. The disciples didn't understand, but they did what they were told, and when it was all over, each disciple carried away more leftovers than he could eat. Seeing what God could do with so little, they were careful not to waste anything, but brought the extra food back to Jesus.

Everything in the world belongs to God, so if He asks you to do something, you don't have to worry that you won't have enough to do the job and take care of your own needs. He'll either multiply what you have or supply more, and you'll be spiritually richer for your obedience. Keep giving what you have to Him, and it will always be enough!

delight |

When has God made it possible for you to do something you thought was impossible?

When have you failed to trust God to provide a way for you to do something He told you to do? What got in the way?

display |

Go into your room and look at all your stuff. Think about what's there and the fact that it all belongs to God. What are you using for His glory to the max? What could you use even more for His glory? What is something that causes you to turn your focus away from God? For each question, write an item below. Then, with your parents' permission, get rid of the item(s) that cause you to lose focus on God.

Glorifies God to the max:

Could be used better for God's glory:

Causes me to turn my focus away from God:

Thank God for all He has provided for you. Ask Him to open your eyes to others' needs and to give you what you need to meet the needs He calls to your attention. Commit to showing the world how generous God is by being generous in His name.

DAY 27

Totally Necessary

discover |

READ LUKE 5:27-32.

*But the Pharisees and their scribes were complaining to [Jesus's] disciples,
"Why do you eat and drink with tax collectors and sinners?" Jesus replied
to them, "It is not those who are healthy who need a doctor, but those who
are sick. I have not come to call the righteous, but sinners to repentance."*
—Luke 5:30-32

We all have sin in our lives—things that don't match God's will or character—and that sin separates us from Him. On our own, we are incapable of finding our way back to God; we are lost. Thankfully, Jesus came to seek and save the lost! Now, all we have to do is put our faith in Jesus's death and resurrection for salvation, and we can live with God forever as His children.

The enemy tries to trick those of us who have been rescued by Jesus into thinking we are better than other people, but the truth is, the only thing that makes us different from anyone else is our faith. This faith doesn't make us better—it is a gift from God (see Eph. 2:8)! No, our faith just makes us blessed and responsible for introducing everyone else to Jesus so they can be rescued, too.

Of course, we can't do that unless we follow Jesus's lead and spend time with people—both those who are looking for God and those whose lifestyles suggest they have either given up the hunt or never began it. Fellowship may not be always be comfortable, but it's absolutely necessary for us and for others!

delight |

How might ignoring a girl who needs Jesus make it harder for her to believe God loves her, too?

Jesus ate with sinners, but the Bible also tells us that bad company corrupts good character (see 1 Cor. 15:33). What can you do to guard yourself against the negative influence of the girls you're trying to minister to?

display |

The next three days will explore the discipline of fellowship. It's easy to pretend you don't know God wants you to reach out to someone if you don't want to do it, but people stand out in our minds for a reason. Make a list of girls who have either been on your mind lately or stand out to you when you see them. Go back through your list. If you know what God wants you to do for or say to any of these girls, write it down and make a specific plan to follow through. Put a question mark next to the girls God hasn't given you specific instructions for yet. Wait and listen for His guidance before acting.

Thank God for sending people to meet your needs and to talk to you about Jesus. Thank Him for the privilege of doing the same for others. Ask God to show you whom He wants you to spend time with and to teach you how to influence the lost without being influenced by them. Follow in Jesus's footsteps and commit to loving people others consider unlovable.

DAY 28

Forever Friends

discover |

READ JOHN 3:1-21.

There was a man from the Pharisees named Nicodemus, a ruler of the Jews. This man came to [Jesus] at night and said, "Rabbi, we know that you are a teacher who has come from God, for no one could perform these signs you do unless God were with him."
—John 3:1-2

If you want healthy friendships that last, you'll need to form them through fellowship built around the gospel of Jesus. Faith in the gospel brings with it the Holy Spirit, who transforms, guides, and empowers us to do God's will for His glory. Because the same Holy Spirit lives in everyone who puts their faith in Jesus's death and resurrection for salvation, children of God are able to connect instantly and forever on a heart level even if they have nothing else in common. It's a miracle, really, and not something to be taken for granted. In fact, we should always look for and take care of the connections we make around the gospel of Jesus.

The Bible says no one comes to God unless the Holy Spirit draws them, so anyone who shows interest in the gospel is a potential forever friend. This being true, we should always respond to their curiosity with truth and fellowship like Jesus did. Nicodemus may not have accepted Jesus's message the first time he heard it, but we do know that he did at some point. He actually cared for Jesus's body after His crucifixion (see John 19:39). No doubt, the fact Jesus was willing to spend time with him had a lot to do with it. Someday, we can ask!

delight |

When has your faith in Jesus helped you connect with someone you wouldn't otherwise have anything in common with?

In what way(s) is the family of God different from biological families?

display |

Remembering that your sisters in Jesus have the same Holy Spirit living in them that you have living in you as a result of your faith in the gospel of Jesus, make a list of friendship-strengthening truths you all should be able to agree on without even having to talk about it. Next, make a list of behaviors you and your sisters in Jesus should be able to expect from one another. Go back through these lists and consider whether or not you have been a good spiritual sister to those around you lately.

Thank God for making deep, lasting friendship possible through Jesus. Ask God to bring into your life friends who are just as committed to His glory as you are. Commit to taking good care of those friendships and to be the kind of spiritual sibling God wants your sisters in Jesus to have.

DAY 29

Remember

discover |

READ MATTHEW 26:26-30.

*As they were eating, Jesus took bread, blessed and broke it, gave it
to the disciples, and said, "Take and eat it; this is my body." Then
he took a cup, and after giving thanks, he gave it to them and
said, "Drink from it, all of you. For this is my blood of the covenant,
which is poured out for many for the forgiveness of sins."*
—*Matthew 26:26–28*

Friends tend to spend time doing the thing(s) that brought them
together in the first place. Musician friends play, listen to, and discuss
music and maybe attend a concert or two. School friends attend school
functions and talk about what happened at school together. Family
friends share memories and observe traditions they have in common.

Likewise, Jesus friends work together to continue His ministry and talk
about what He has done for them. One way Jesus friends deepen their
friendship is by observing the Lord's Supper, an ordinance that reminds
us of the sacrifice Jesus made on the cross, what it has to do with us, and
the everlasting bond that we share as brothers and sisters in Christ.

The Bible tells us to prepare our hearts before we take the Lord's Supper.
This involves confessing our sin and making peace with our brothers and
sisters in Jesus. Once we have made God's glory our first priority again,
we can come together and remember. Jesus not only established the
church, but just thinking about Him also keeps it healthy!

delight |

How does thinking about what Jesus did for you affect the way you feel toward people? The way you act toward them?

What other spiritual practices make you feel close to your sisters in Jesus?

display |

Imagine you are taking the Lord's Supper today. To do it as Jesus instructed, we need to prepare ourselves. Outline what steps you would need to take to be prepared to take the Lord's Supper today. Then, go ahead and take those actions even though you aren't planning to take the Lord's Supper today. After all, the right time to do the right thing is always right now!

Thank God for sending you a Savior who not only brings you and your spiritual siblings together, but holds you together. Confess any failure on your part to sacrifice for them the way Jesus sacrificed for you. Commit to work to maintain unity in the church at all times so people will want to know Jesus for themselves.

DAY 30

Give and You Will Receive!

discover |

READ MARK 12:29-31.

"Love the Lord your God with all your heart, with all your
soul, with all your mind, and with all your strength."
—Mark 12:30

The Bible tell us that we prove our love for God by obeying His commands. This being true, we can't love God unless we know what His commands are. We discover what His commands are and understand what they mean through the inward, outward, and corporate spiritual disciplines Jesus practiced: prayer, fasting, Bible study, simplicity, solitude, submission, service, worship, stewardship, and fellowship.

Affection for God isn't bad, but it can be fickle if we're not careful. True love for God—the kind that proves He is unchanging and worthy—requires intentional effort and every part of our being. We love God with our heart by deciding He is more important than anything or anyone else. We love God with our soul by making choices that gamble our spiritual safety on the truth of His Word. We love God with our mind by dedicating its thoughts to the advancement of His kingdom. We love God with our strength by using our bodies to do His will. We do all this for His glory, not ours.

Practicing spiritual disciplines doesn't guarantee we won't make any mistakes, but it does increase our chances of getting more things right. What's more, it makes deeper intimacy with God possible, settling our spirits and stirring up joy as we give and receive love! What could be better than that?

Cultivate

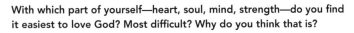

delight |

With which part of yourself—heart, soul, mind, strength—do you find it easiest to love God? Most difficult? Why do you think that is?

Which of the spiritual disciplines you've studied this month do you need to work on so you can get to know and represent God better?

display |

Under each word below, list the ways that you currently love God by obeying Him with that part of yourself. Consider how practicing each of the spiritual disciplines you studied about this month—prayer, fasting, Bible study, simplicity, solitude, submission, service, worship, stewardship, and fellowship—could help you love Him more deeply in each of these four areas.

Heart   **Soul**   **Mind**   **Strength**

Thank God for giving you the tools you need to know Him better and represent Him well. Tell Him all the reasons He deserves to be glorified. Ask Him to forgive you for the times you didn't show the world who He really is or give them reason to believe what He's done for them. Commit to making a conscious effort to love Him with every part of yourself.

HOW TO JOURNAL YOUR PRAYERS

You probably spend a lot of time writing. You put your thoughts and ideas out there in social media posts, you do schoolwork, and maybe even write in a devotional book like this one. But we don't often stop to think about the less visible ways writing benefits us. Writing can help us think more clearly, unravel our emotions, remember important details, reduce stress, be creative, and of course, communicate. Since prayer is how we communicate with God, writing can even help us practice this spiritual discipline. Really, there are only two rules to this practice: be reverent and be real.

Follow the guide below—modified from the ACTS prayer model: adoration, confession, thanksgiving, and supplication—to help you journal your own prayer today.

Admire God. Praise Him for who He is. Here are a few of His attributes to help you get started. Highlight the one(s) you resonate with most today—or write in your own!

- **Love**
- **Grace**
- **Mercy**
- **Kindness**
- **Compassion**
- **Eternality (He has always existed; He always will)**

- **Sovereignty (Nothing is beyond His control)**
- **Justice**
- **Holiness**
- **Righteousness**
- **_____**

Call out sin in your life and seek forgiveness. Read the following prayerful confessions in Scripture. Circle the one that stands out to you.

- **Daniel 9:4-19**
- **Psalm 32:5**
- **Psalm 51**
- **Luke 18:9-14**

Think of the gifts God has given you and thank Him for each one. These questions might help:

- Who has God placed around you who supports and encourages you?
- What simple things are you thankful for? Big things?
- Where has God provided for you to live, go to school, work, hang out with friends, and so on?
- When has God worked out the details for something that would've otherwise been impossible, or when has He provided in an unexpected way?
- Why and how are you able to have a relationship with God?

Seek God. In Mark 10:51, a blind man recognized who Jesus was and asked for mercy. Jesus responded by asking the man, "What do you want me to do for you?" Take some time to answer that question.

Now, look back at the words you've highlighted, Scripture passages you've circled, and questions you've answered. Use those ideas to help you journal your prayer. Use a blank sheet of paper or consider starting your own prayer journal.

WHY WE NEED SPACE FOR SOLITUDE (AND WHY IT'S OKAY)

God created us for relationships with Him and others, and throughout this devotional, we've discovered how to deepen our relationship with God through spiritual disciplines. But here's the thing: sometimes, to create space for this closeness with God, we have to make time to step away from everything else. We need solitude, silence, and rest to get to know Jesus and to get to know who God has designed us to be.

When we get away from everything, our eyes are cleared to see that He is everything and He provides all that we need. Jesus modeled this act of creating space away from the noise and busyness of life to connect with God—when He was tired, grieving, and even when He was asking God if there was any other way than the cross. Jesus usually went somewhere peaceful (like a mountain or a garden), He went at the end of the day (His work accomplished for the time being), and He prayed.

You might not be able to go for a hike and find a stunning overlook or even go to a local park, but you can create space for solitude in your own backyard, or even in your own room. (Note: Please be sure to do this safely. If you would like to spend time alone outside of your own home, seek guidance from your parents or guardians.)

On a scale of one to ten, how often do you spend time alone?

1	2	3	4	5	6	7	8	9	10
Never			**Sometimes**				**Several times per day**		

Now, how often do you spend time alone, not on your phone?

1	2	3	4	5	6	7	8	9	10
Never			**Sometimes**				**Several times per day**		

Okay, so sometimes it seems like there's just no escaping the screens, right? So, be intentional. Put your phone on silent or turn it off completely and set it out of sight (in another room if you can). Grab a Bible, a notebook or journal, and a pen. Now make a plan.

Where can you go that's peaceful?

When is the best time of day for you to "get away" to spend time alone with God?

What will you pray for while you're there?

Who will you tell where you are if you decide to go somewhere outside the house?

This plan might change each day, and that's okay. What's important is to make solitude—a time to rest and be refreshed—a daily practice, even if it's just ten minutes. Creating space specifically to connect with God is a simple, yet powerful way we can grow in our faith.

Notes